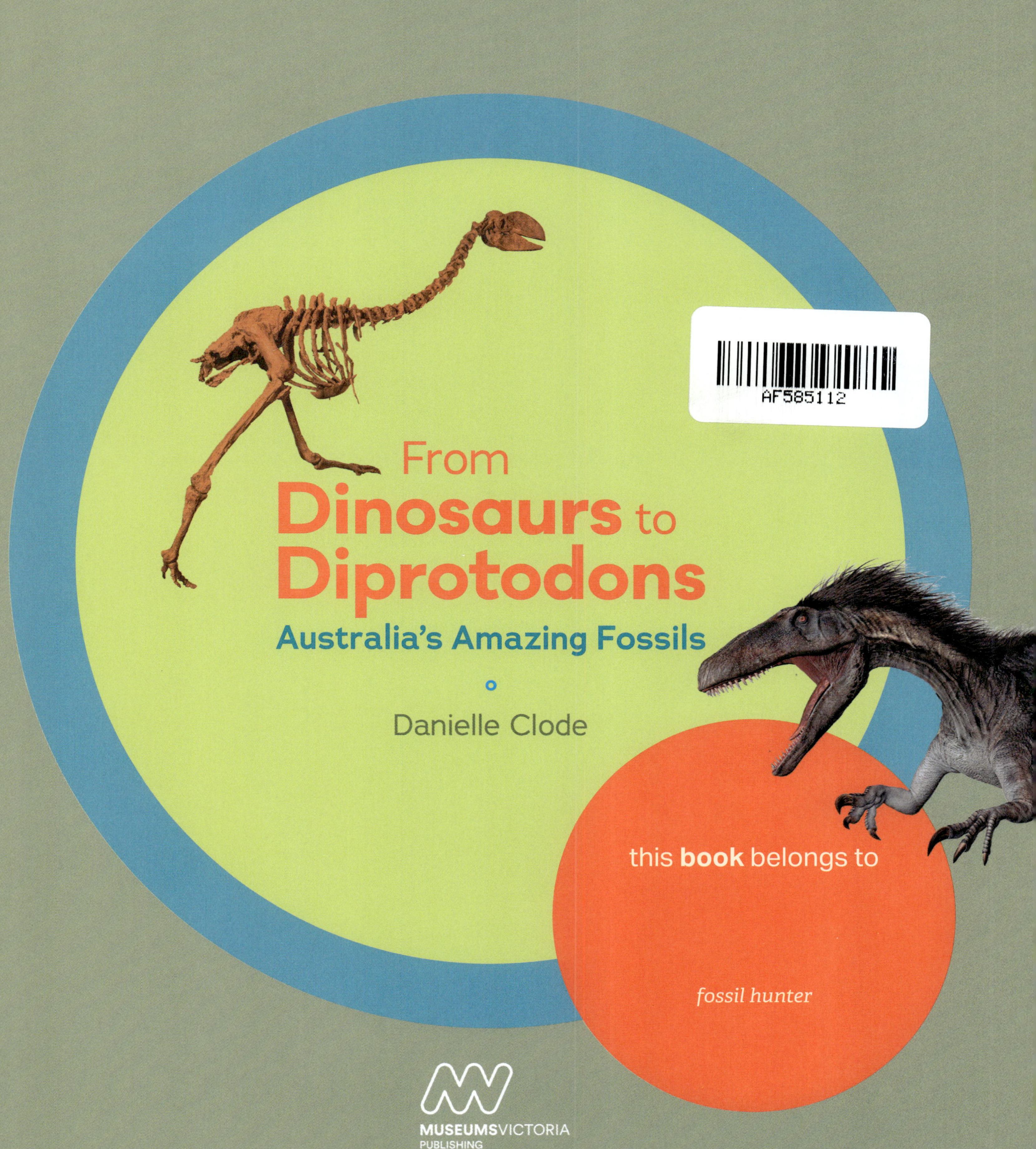

# From Dinosaurs to Diprotodons

## Australia's Amazing Fossils

Danielle Clode

this **book** belongs to

*fossil hunter*



MUSEUMSVICTORIA
PUBLISHING

# Contents

# Amazing Australian Fossils

Australia has many fossil sites. We have fossils of the earliest animals on Earth and of the largest dinosaurs. We even have fossils of giant megafauna that lived alongside humans. Come and find the best places to see fossils around Australia.

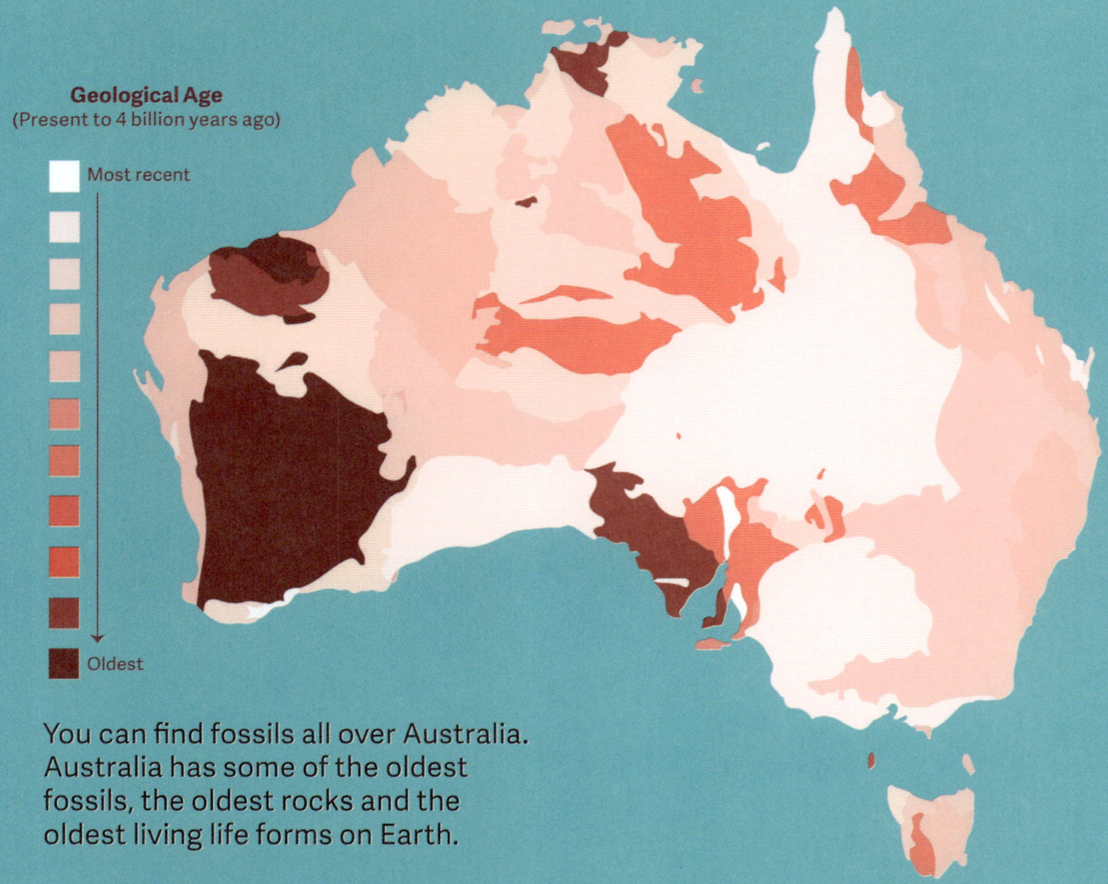


You can find fossils all over Australia. Australia has some of the oldest fossils, the oldest rocks and the oldest living life forms on Earth.

**Stromatolites** are living fossils. Stromatolite means 'layered rock'. They grow from layers of blue-green algae. Fossil stromatolites are up to 3.5 billion years old. Today, they live in shallow, salty bays in Western Australia.
stroh-MAT-oh-lights

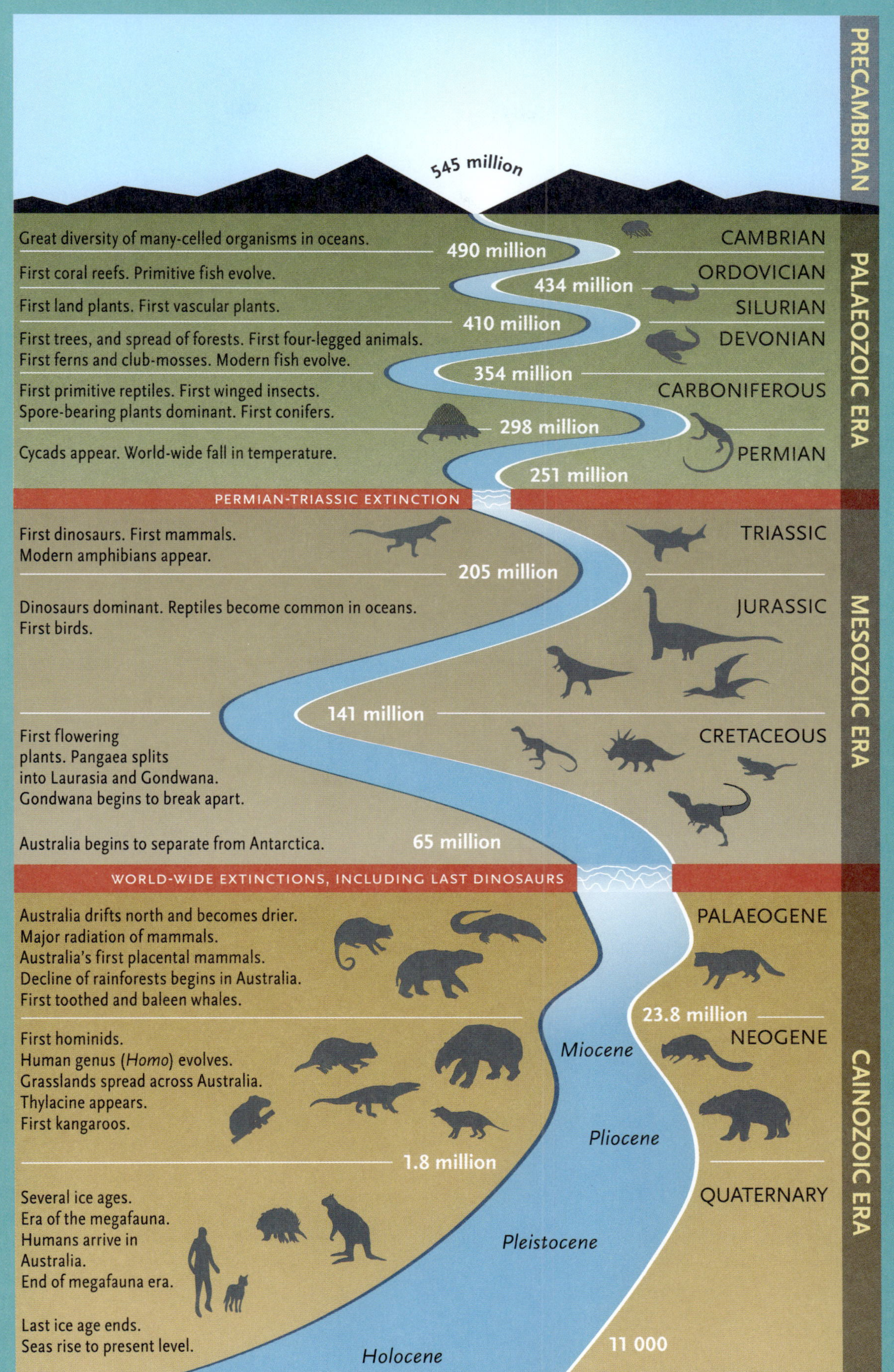
PRECAMBRIAN
545 million
Great diversity of many-celled organisms in oceans.
490 million
CAMBRIAN
First coral reefs. Primitive fish evolve.
434 million
ORDOVICIAN
First land plants. First vascular plants.
SILURIAN
410 million
First trees, and spread of forests. First four-legged animals.
First ferns and club-mosses. Modern fish evolve.
DEVONIAN
354 million
First primitive reptiles. First winged insects.
Spore-bearing plants dominant. First conifers.
CARBONIFEROUS
298 million
Cycads appear. World-wide fall in temperature.
PERMIAN
251 million
PALAEOZOIC ERA
PERMIAN-TRIASSIC EXTINCTION
First dinosaurs. First mammals.
Modern amphibians appear.
TRIASSIC
205 million
Dinosaurs dominant. Reptiles become common in oceans.
First birds.
JURASSIC
141 million
First flowering
plants. Pangaea splits
into Laurasia and Gondwana.
Gondwana begins to break apart.
CRETACEOUS
Australia begins to separate from Antarctica.
65 million
MESOZOIC ERA
WORLD-WIDE EXTINCTIONS, INCLUDING LAST DINOSAURS
Australia drifts north and becomes drier.
Major radiation of mammals.
Australia's first placental mammals.
Decline of rainforests begins in Australia.
First toothed and baleen whales.
PALAEOGENE
23.8 million
First hominids.
Human genus (Homo) evolves.
Grasslands spread across Australia.
Thylacine appears.
First kangaroos.
Miocene
NEOGENE
Pliocene
1.8 million
Several ice ages.
Era of the megafauna.
Humans arrive in
Australia.
End of megafauna era.
Pleistocene
QUATERNARY
Last ice age ends.
Seas rise to present level.
Holocene
11 000
CAINOZOIC ERA

# Fossicking for Fossils

Fossils are sometimes formed when an animal dies in water like this **nautilus**. Water covers the body with sand or mud. Over a long time, this sediment turns to rock. The body leaves a print in the rock, creating a fossil.

## WHAT ARE THEY?

Fossils are traces of past life preserved in rocks. Animal fossils can be piles of bones or bones that have turned into rock. Sometimes plants and animals are preserved in ice or in peat bogs. Footprints, eggs, shells and even droppings can be fossils.

The weather has exposed this ***Diprotodon*** skeleton from a dry lake bed. Lake Callabonna in South Australia is much drier than it was in the past.
digh-PROH-toh-don

These footprints were made by one of the first animals to walk on land. This **tetrapod** was like a fish with legs. It made these prints about 360 million years ago in Genoa, Victoria.
TET-raa-pod

**Fossil insects** are sometimes preserved in amber. Amber is the fossilised sap from trees.

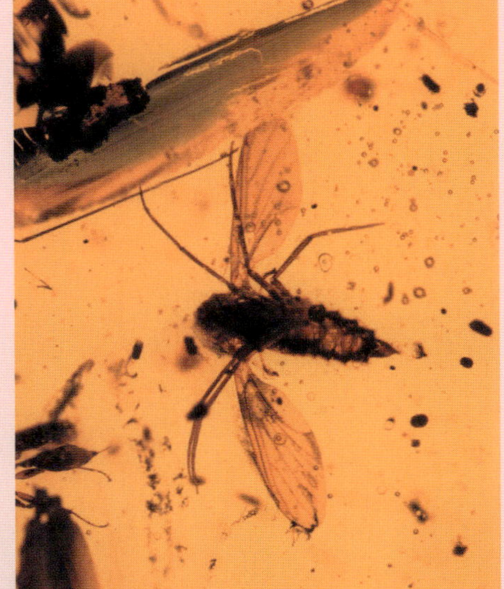

These **fossil shells** have been exposed on the sea-cliffs of Maria Island, Tasmania. Fossils can also be found in areas around Hobart.

This skeleton of the marsupial 'lion' ***Thylacoleo*** was found in the Nullarbor Caves. Skeletons are often scattered by water or scavengers. Complete skeletons are sometimes found undisturbed in caves.
THIGH-lak-oh-LEE-oh

## Did you know?

**You can hunt for your own fossils in many parts of Australia. Ask your local fossil centre or museum for advice on safe places to find fossils. Fossil pirates sometimes sell Australian fossils overseas illegally. If you find a fossil you can take it to your local natural history museum and they will help you identify it.**

## WHERE ARE THEY?

Fossils can be found in many different places. Fossils are often found in caves. They can be found in cliffs where the sea has washed away the rock face. Or they can be found in remote areas where few people visit. In this book, we will see some of Australia's most exciting fossil sites.

# The Age of Megafauna

## NARACOORTE CAVES

***Palorchestes azael***
used its flexible nose and long tongue to eat leaves.
pal-orr-KEST-eez az-EEL

### WHAT ARE THEY?

Megafauna are large extinct animals from the last ice age. Australia did not have giant mammoths or sabre-toothed cats. Instead, Australia had giant marsupials and reptiles. Most megafauna died out about 40,000 to 45,000 years ago.

Stood 2.5 metres tall

Could rotate its shoulders to reach into trees

### Did you know?

**In 1969 some cavers discovered a cavern at Naracoorte filled with fossils. These animals fell through a hole in the roof and were trapped. The Naracoorte Caves are now a World Heritage fossil site.**

***Procoptodon goliah***
was a large kangaroo quite different from modern kangaroos.
proh-COP-toh-don go-LIGH-uh

Called a 'short-faced kangaroo' because of its flat muzzle

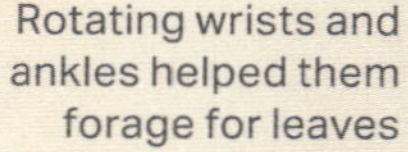

Rotating wrists and ankles helped them forage for leaves

***Propleopus oscillans***
was a kangaroo that ate meat.
prop-LEE-oh-pus OS-il-ans

This ***Diprotodon*** skull has flat molar teeth for grinding food. The large front teeth cut through plant material.

## WHERE ARE THEY?

You can visit the Wonambi Fossil Centre at Naracoorte. Explore some of the caves to find out more about Australia's megafauna.

***Diprotodon optatum***
was a giant marsupial herbivore. It was the size of a rhinoceros and may have lived in a herd.
digh-PROH-toh-don op-TAA-tum

***Latagallina naracoortensis***
was twice as big as modern brush turkeys. It buried its eggs in warm sand.
la-ta-GALL-een-ah NA-rar-coor-TEN-sis

# Polar Dinosaurs

## DINOSAUR COVE

### WHAT ARE THEY?

Dinosaur Cove was once a rift valley joining Australia and Antarctica. Small fossil fragments were washed down a river. Some of these fossils were from small dinosaurs. Some of the first known Australian dinosaurs were found here and at Inverloch.

The size of a turkey

Parts of ***Leaellynasaura***'s brain were unusually large and left an imprint on the skull.

Bird-like (ornithischian) hips

Large parts of the brain devoted to vision and movement

Big eyes

### Did you know?

**Dinosaur Cove used to be much colder and closer to the South Pole than it is today. It was dark for several months of the year. Despite the cold there were lush forests along the rivers, filled with insects, fish and turtles.**

***Leaellynasaura amicagraphica*** was a small two-legged dinosaur. It probably ate plants and insects in the forests.
lee-EL-in-aa-SOOR-aa AM-ik-aa-GRAF-ik-aa

Cambrian | Ordovician | Silurian | Devonian | Carboniferous | Permian | Triassic | Jurassic | Cretaceous | Paleogene | Neogene

−500 million years | −400 | −300 | −200 | −100 | 0

Giant predatory amphibians called **temnospondyls** had nearly disappeared by the Cretaceous. The Australian species *Koolasuchus cleelandi* was the last species known.
TEM-noh-spon-dil / kool-A-suk-us clee-LAND-igh

## WHERE ARE THEY?

Dinosaur Cove is hard to get to. But there are many other good sites for finding fossils along the Victorian coast. You can find out more at the Bunurong Environment Centre in Inverloch and at Melbourne Museum.

↗

***Atlascopcosaurus loadsi*** was named after the company that helped excavate the site. Many small dinosaur bones have been found here.
AT-las-COP-co-SOOR-us LOHD-zigh

Tiny mammals the size of mice, like ***Bishops whitmorei***, lived alongside the dinosaurs.
BISH-ops WIT-moor-igh

***Qantassaurus intrepidus*** was a plant-eating dinosaur found near Inverloch. It was fast-moving and the size of a gazelle.
KWON-taa-SOOR-us in-TREP-id-us

# Ancient Whales and Deadly Dolphins

## TORQUAY COAST

### WHAT ARE THEY?

The surf coast near Torquay contains many fossils of early whales. You can also find fossil shells and crabs as well as the bones and teeth of sharks and fish.

This long-beaked ***Waipatiid*** dolphin was an ancestor of the modern Ganges River dolphin.
wy-PAT-ee-id

### Did you know?

**These early whale fossils tell us how baleen whales evolved and lost their teeth. Torquay is one of the most important sites for fossil whales in Australia.**

A surfer found this ***Janjucetus*** whale skull at Jan Juc beach.

***Prosqualodon*** was similar to modern dolphins but with protruding teeth.
PRO-skwal-oh-don

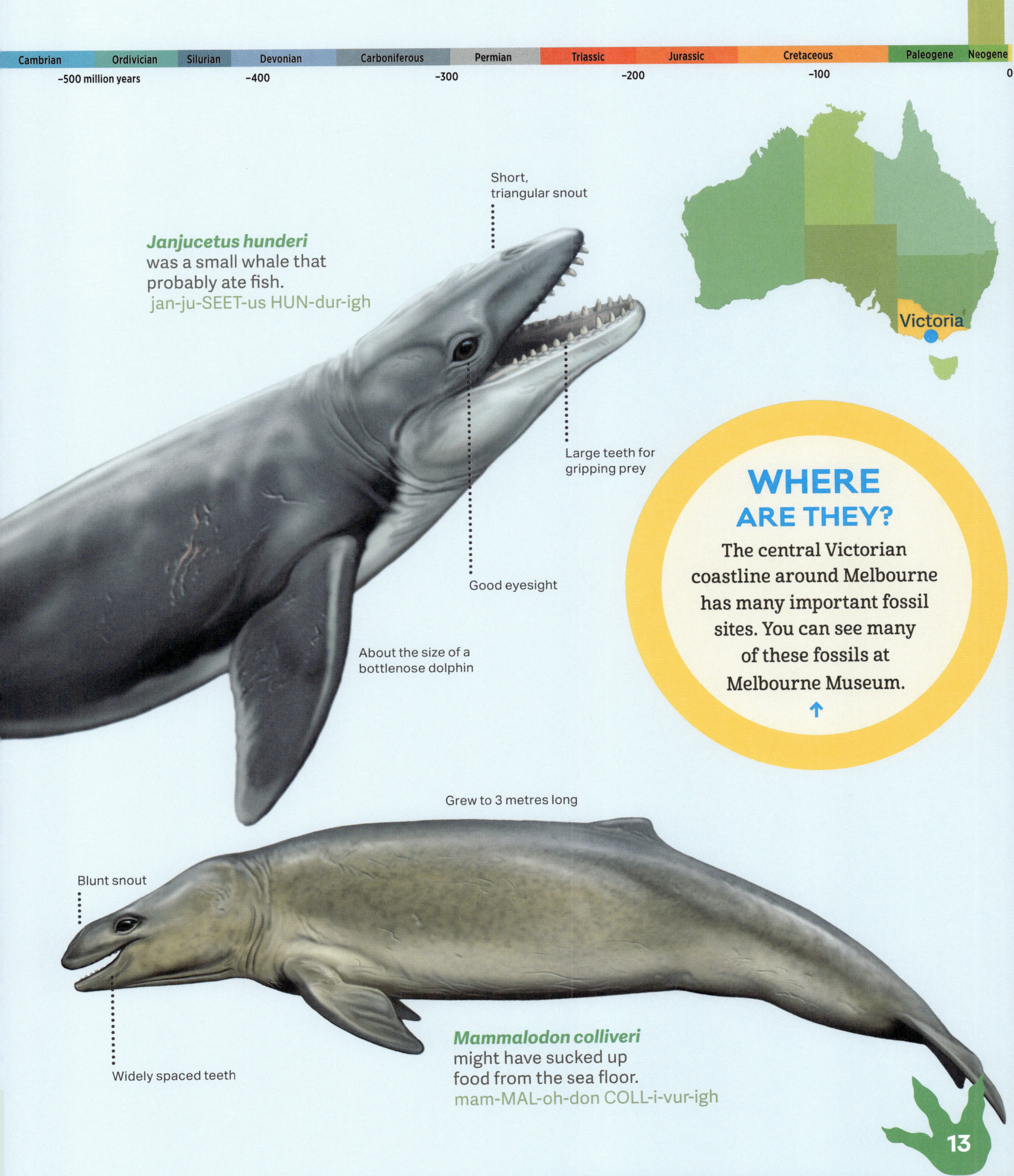


***Janjucetus hunderi*** was a small whale that probably ate fish.
jan-ju-SEET-us HUN-dur-igh

## WHERE ARE THEY?

The central Victorian coastline around Melbourne has many important fossil sites. You can see many of these fossils at Melbourne Museum.

***Mammalodon colliveri*** might have sucked up food from the sea floor.
mam-MAL-oh-don COLL-i-vur-igh

# Giant Sharks and Toothy Birds

## BEAUMARIS

The teeth of the giant shark ***Carcharocles megalodon*** are sometimes found on Beaumaris Beach.
Kar-KA-roh-kleez MEG-a-lo-don

*Megalodon* means 'big tooth'. *Megalodon* teeth are the largest known shark teeth (17 cm)

### WHAT ARE THEY?

Fossils found at Beaumaris range from large whales to small sea urchins. The site is important for studying the evolution of ancient penguins, sea turtles and land animals.

***Pelagornis*** was a large seabird with a wingspan of 5–6 metres and jagged 'teeth' along its beak. It was found at Beaumaris.
pel-a-GOR-nis

*Livyatan* had the biggest teeth of any non-tusked animal (up to 36 cm)

Cambrian
Ordivician
Silurian
Devonian
Carboniferous
Permian
Triassic
Jurassic
Cretaceous
Paleogene
Neogene
-500 million years
-400
-300
-200
-100
0
WHERE ARE THEY?
Beaumaris is a coastal suburb of Melbourne. It is one of the richest marine fossil sites in Australia.
Victoria
Did you know?
Beaumaris is being considered as a World Heritage fossil site to protect it from coastal development.
Livyatan
was a giant sperm whale and a fearsome predator.
le-VIGH-aa-tan
Skull 3 metres long
Largest known teeth – up to 36 centimetres long
Hunted large prey like sharks, whales and squid
Weighed 40 tonnes
Up to 18 metres long
Pseudaptenodytes macraei
was one of many prehistoric penguins that once lived in Australia.
sood-ap-TEN-oh-digh-teez ma-KRAY-igh

# Caves of Prehistoric Giants

## WELLINGTON CAVES

***Bohra paulae***
was a large tree kangaroo named after a local Aboriginal legend.
BORR-a PORR-lee

Three times heavier than modern tree kangaroos

Long, wide back feet for tree climbing

Large, heavy tail for balance

### WHAT ARE THEY?

The Wellington Caves contain many megafauna fossils. Aboriginal people called them bunyips. Early explorers thought these giant animals died in a flood. Charles Darwin noticed that the giant fossils were like living species. Fossils like these helped him understand evolution.

Heavy limbs and body like modern Komodo dragons

The largest lizard ever, at over 5 metres long

### Did you know?

**The Wellington Caves were one of the first places where fossils were studied in Australia. A farmer, George Ranken, brought the explorer Thomas Mitchell here in 1830. Ranken tied his climbing rope to a giant thigh bone.**

Giant wombats grew to the size of a large pig, like this ***Phascolonus gigas***.
FAZ-col-O-nus JI-gas

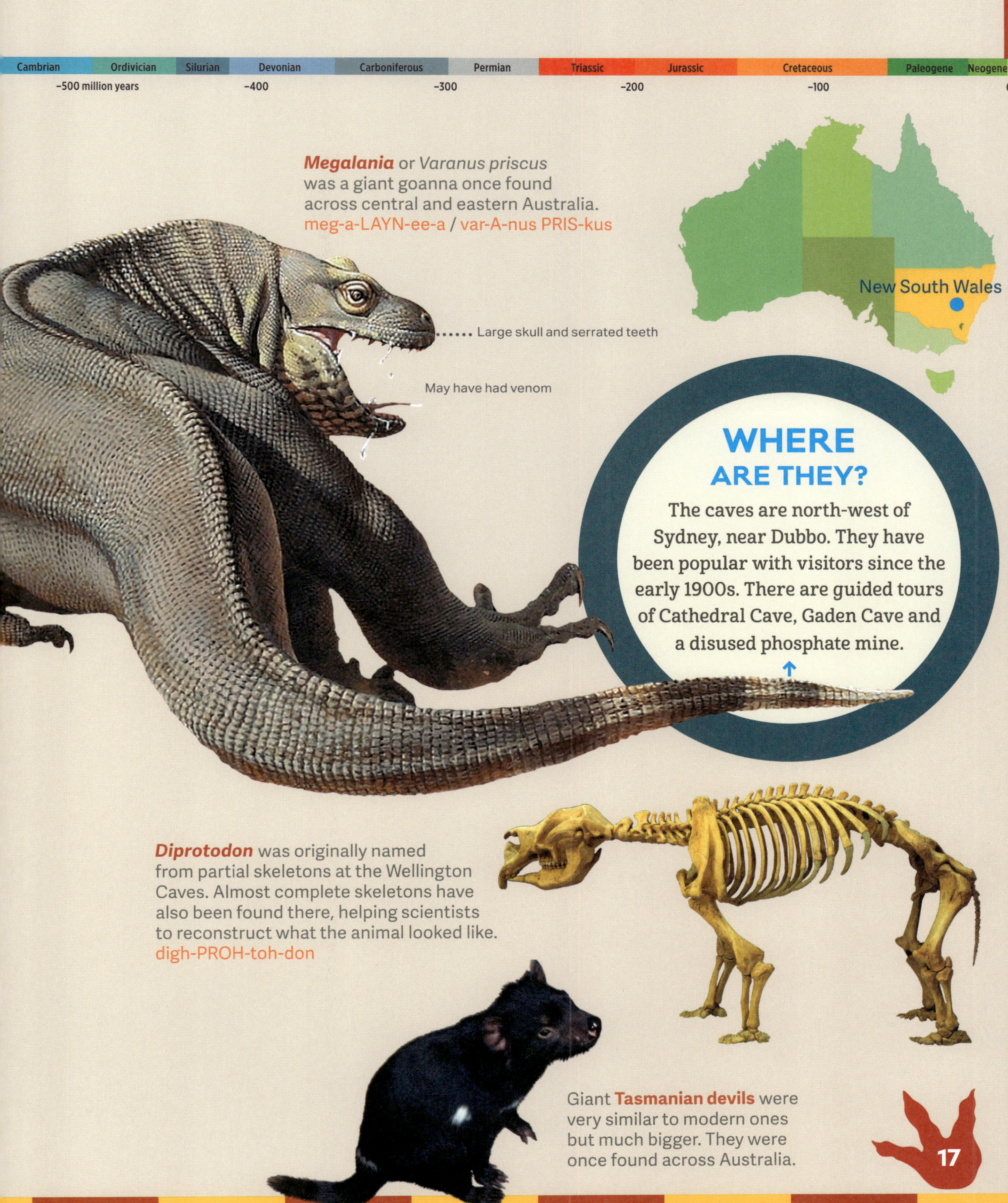


***Megalania*** or *Varanus priscus* was a giant goanna once found across central and eastern Australia. meg-a-LAYN-ee-a / var-A-nus PRIS-kus

## WHERE ARE THEY?

The caves are north-west of Sydney, near Dubbo. They have been popular with visitors since the early 1900s. There are guided tours of Cathedral Cave, Gaden Cave and a disused phosphate mine.

***Diprotodon*** was originally named from partial skeletons at the Wellington Caves. Almost complete skeletons have also been found there, helping scientists to reconstruct what the animal looked like. digh-PROH-toh-don

Giant **Tasmanian devils** were very similar to modern ones but much bigger. They were once found across Australia.

# The Lake of Armoured Fish

## CANOWINDRA

### WHAT ARE THEY?

Millions of years ago a lake dried out, trapping the fish that lived there. The fish were perfectly preserved in sediment at the bottom of the lake.

Long, cylindrical body with fins at the rear for short bursts of speed

***Mandageria*** was a top predator. It probably ambushed its prey like pike do today.
man-daa-JE-ree-aa

About as long as a small person – 1.6 metres long.

Large, flat head

Pointed teeth and fangs

## Did you know?

**When these fish were alive, Australia was part of Gondwana. Canowindra lay near the equator.**
gon-DWAA-naa

***Bothriolepis*** was a very common fish with bony armour.
both-ree-oh-LEE-pis

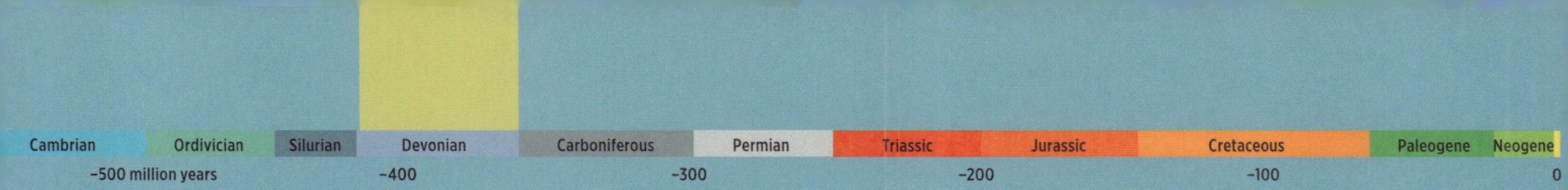

Cambrian | Ordovician | Silurian | Devonian | Carboniferous | Permian | Triassic | Jurassic | Cretaceous | Paleogene | Neogene

-500 million years | -400 | -300 | -200 | -100 | 0

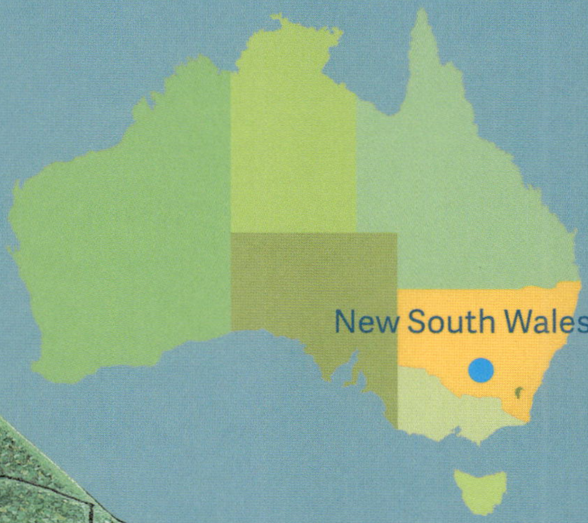

New South Wales

Fossils of ***Groenlandaspis*** are found in Greenland, North America and Australia.
grin-lund-AS-pis

A bony body shield with a fin-like ridge

Half a metre long

Fins protected by bony ridges

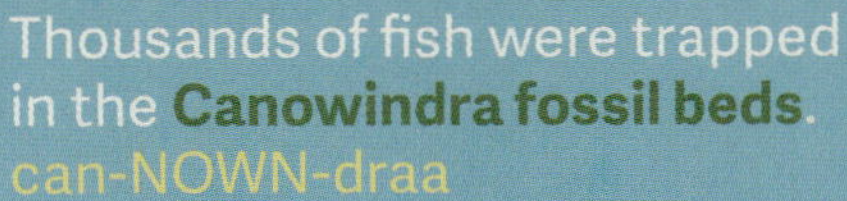
Thousands of fish were trapped in the **Canowindra fossil beds**.
can-NOWN-draa

## WHERE ARE THEY?

You can see these fossils at the Age of Fishes Museum in Canowindra. Canowindra is 300 km west of Sydney.

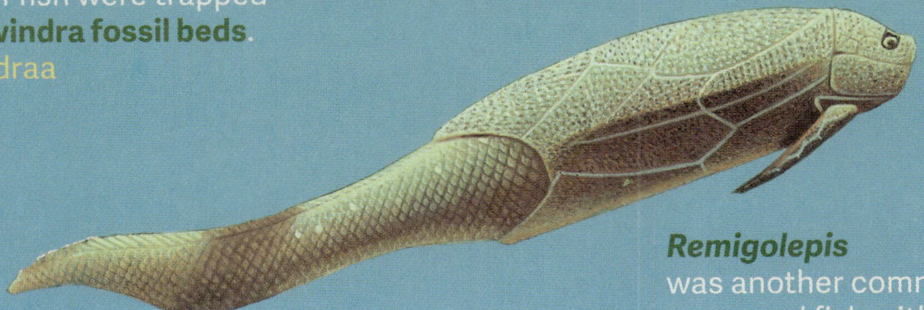

***Remigolepis***
was another common armoured fish with an oar-like fin.
rem-ee-goh-LEE-pis

# Dinosaurs of Lightning Claws

## LIGHTNING RIDGE

**WHAT ARE THEY?**

Lightning Ridge has a wide range of plant and animal fossils. There are dinosaur, marine reptile and platypus fossils here.

Many fossil **lungfish** are almost identical to lungfish living in Queensland rivers today.

***Muttaburrasaurus*** was a large plant-eating ornithopod dinosaur found across New South Wales and Queensland. mut-a-bu-ra-SOOR-us

***Steropodon galmani*** was a very early type of platypus. sterr-o-POH-don GAL-man-igh

Fossil fragments of small ornithopod dinosaurs, like ***Fulgurotherium***, have been found at Lightning Ridge. FULL-gur-o-THEER-ee-um

## Did you know?

**Many of the fossils at Lightning Ridge are made of opal. Opals are common gems in parts of Australia once covered by an inland sea. Opals are rare elsewhere.**

## WHERE ARE THEY?

Lightning Ridge is just south of the Queensland border. You can search for your own opals and fossils or explore the mines.

↗

The megaraptor '**Lightning Claw**' is the biggest predatory dinosaur found in Australia so far. It was named for its large, hooked claws. MEG-a-RAP-toor

***Kollikodon*** means 'bun tooth'. Scientists thought these platypus teeth looked like hot cross buns. KOLL-ee-koh-don

# Thingodonts and Fangaroos

## RIVERSLEIGH

***Yalkaparidon*** was a very strange animal. It was nicknamed 'Thingodonta' because it is so different from other animals.
YAL-kaa-parr-ee-don

### WHAT ARE THEY?

Riversleigh has many mammal fossils. Hundreds of different species have been found here. It is a World Heritage fossil site.

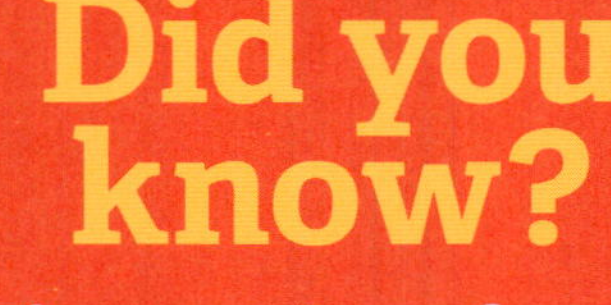

***Ekaltadeta ima*** was a carnivorous giant rat-kangaroo.
EK-al-ta-DEE-ta EE-ma

### Did you know?

**The ancestors of many Australian animals are found at Riversleigh. These include kangaroos, koalas, platypuses and possums.**

This tiny skull (life-size) belonged to ***Yarala burchfieldi***, one of the oldest known bandicoots. It was the size of a mouse.
YA-ra-laa burch-FEEL-digh

***Balbaroo fangaroo*** was named for its long canine teeth.
BAL-baa-roo FANG-aa-roo

## WHERE ARE THEY?

Riversleigh is in the outback of north Queensland. You can see the fossils at the Riversleigh Fossil Centre in Mount Isa.

The ***Emuary*** seems to have been the ancestor of both the cassowary and the emu.
EM-yoo-arr-ee

Early koalas like ***Nimiokoala greystanesi*** have been found at Riversleigh.
NIM-ee-oh-koh-AA-laa gray-stan-EE-zigh

# The Mighty Titanosaurs

## EROMANGA

Long neck for browsing in trees

### WHAT ARE THEY?

Titanosaur **sauropods** are found all over the world. Several titanosaur fossils have been found in Queensland over the last twenty years. The Eromanga titanosaurs are amongst the biggest in the world. Eromanga also has megafauna, plant and aquatic fossils.

SOOR-oh-pod

**Titanosaurs** like 'Cooper' and 'George' were bigger than a bus. They were even bigger than a semi-trailer.
tigh-TAN-oh-soor

Flowering plants were rare. Instead, plants like gingkoes, clubmosses and horsetails grew on the forest floor. **Ferns** were also common.

Cooper's **femur** or thigh bone is as big as a person. It is 1.9 metres long.

Titanosaurs fed in the conifer forests. These ***Araucaria*** conifers were related to modern Bunya pines.
a-ro-CAIR-ee-a

The conifer forests contained many other plants including long-living, slow growing **cycads**. SIGH-cads

## WHERE ARE THEY?

You can see titanosaur fossils at the Eromanga Natural History Museum in south-west Queensland. It is close to the border between Queensland, South Australia, New South Wales and the Northern Territory.

## Did you know?

**The only animal bigger than the titanosaurs is the blue whale. Most of the titanosaurs at Eromanga are known only from a few bones. They have not been classified as species yet.**

Large **sauropod footprints** have also been found at Eromanga, like these found along the beaches near Broome in Western Australia (with 30 cm ruler). SOOR-oh-pod

# Megaraptors and the Big Stampede

## WINTON

***Isisfordia***
was a small crocodile.
It was the first of the mekosuchine crocodiles.
IGH-sis-foor-DEE-aa / MEE-koh-SOO-kighn

### WHAT ARE THEY?

The footprints of a dinosaur stampede can be seen at Lark Quarry. The fossils of titanosaurs and predatory megaraptors have also been found nearby.

### Did you know?

**The Lark Quarry dinosaur stampede is thought to be the only fossilised dinosaur stampede in the world. There are 4000 dinosaur footprints from a herd of small emu-sized ornithopods and chicken-sized coelurosaurs. Large tyrannosaur footprints cross the smaller tracks.**

OOR-nith-oh-pods / sel-YOO-roh-soors

Stood 2 metres tall and 1.5 metres at hip

Up to 5 metres long

Large 30-centimetre-long killing claws

'Banjo' was a megaraptor called ***Australovenator wintonensis***.
Its name means 'Winton's southern hunter'.
OS-traa-loh-ven-aa-toor win-ton-EN-sis

| Cambrian | Ordivician | Silurian | Devonian | Carboniferous | Permian | Triassic | Jurassic | Cretaceous | Paleogene | Neogene |
|---|---|---|---|---|---|---|---|---|---|---|

-500 million years -400 -300 -200 -100 0

The **Lark Quarry Dinosaur Stampede** National Monument contains the most concentrated set of dinosaur footprints in the world.

'Matilda' was a titanosaur called ***Diamantinasaurus matildae***. This fossil was trapped in mud with the megaraptor 'Banjo'.
digh-man-TEEN-aa-SOOR-us mat-IL-dee

Splayed foot bones for carrying weight

Thumb claw for defence

Named after Banjo Paterson's 'Waltzing Matilda', which was written near Winton

## WHERE ARE THEY?

The Lark Quarry Dinosaur Stampede National Monument and the Australian Age of Dinosaurs Museum are near Winton in central Queensland. Dinosaur footprints can also be seen in Queensland in the Mount Morgan gold mine and in Carnarvon Gorge near Rolleston.

Many small to medium **Theropod dinosaurs** have been found near Winton. Theropods are the ancestors of modern birds.
THERR-oh-pod

# Beasts of the Inland Sea

## HUGHENDEN and RICHMOND

Lots of big teeth

Large head (2.5 metres long) and a short, strong neck

***Kronosaurus*** was a large apex predator that grew up to 10 metres long.
KROH-noh-SOOR-us

Stiff, well-muscled body for speed

Air-breathing

Wing-like flippers

## Did you know?

**In the age of the dinosaurs, outback Australia was flooded by the Eromanga sea. After this cold, shallow sea disappeared, the fossils of many marine animals were turned into colourful opals.**

## WHAT ARE THEY?

The animals of Australia's inland sea included long-necked plesiosaurs and short-necked pliosaurs. Schools of fish and sharks looked similar to ones today. The many species of squid-like ammonites and belemnites no longer exist in modern oceans.

PLEEZ-ee-oh-soors / PLIGH-oh-soors

***Ammonites*** were very abundant in the Cretaceous but are now extinct.
AM-on-ights

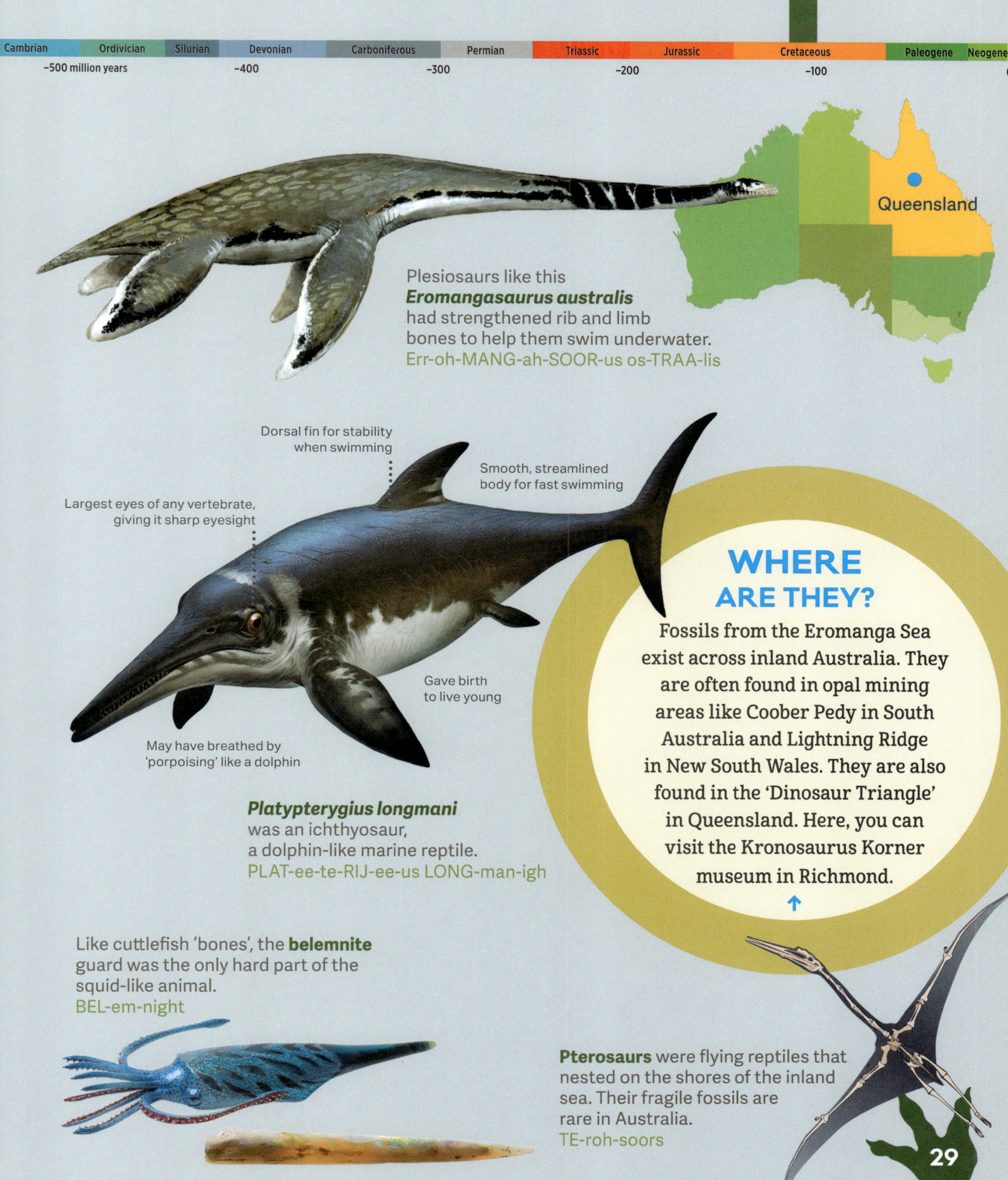


Plesiosaurs like this ***Eromangasaurus australis*** had strengthened rib and limb bones to help them swim underwater.
Err-oh-MANG-ah-SOOR-us os-TRAA-lis

***Platypterygius longmani*** was an ichthyosaur, a dolphin-like marine reptile.
PLAT-ee-te-RIJ-ee-us LONG-man-igh

## WHERE ARE THEY?

Fossils from the Eromanga Sea exist across inland Australia. They are often found in opal mining areas like Coober Pedy in South Australia and Lightning Ridge in New South Wales. They are also found in the 'Dinosaur Triangle' in Queensland. Here, you can visit the Kronosaurus Korner museum in Richmond.

Like cuttlefish 'bones', the **belemnite** guard was the only hard part of the squid-like animal.
BEL-em-night

**Pterosaurs** were flying reptiles that nested on the shores of the inland sea. Their fragile fossils are rare in Australia.
TE-roh-soors

# **Life** with the **Thunderbirds**

## ALCOOTA

***Wakaleo vanderleuri***
was one of many thylacine predators in the Miocene.
WAK-a-lee-oh van-dur-LOO-ree-igh

Teeth modified for stabbing and slicing meat

Strong jaws for crushing bone

Marsupial pouch for young joeys

Claws for gripping prey and climbing trees

### WHAT ARE THEY?

The Alcoota bone beds were formed when many animals were trapped at drying lakes. The bones of 3000 animals have been found at Alcoota. At the time, the area was covered in open woodlands.

***Kolopsis torus***
was a sheep-sized zygomaturine that browsed in large herds.
KOL-op-sis TOOR-us / zigh-goh-MAT-yoo-reen

***Palorchestes painei***
was a marsupial about the size of a small horse. It had a long tongue for reaching leaves.
PAL-oor-kes-teez PAY-nee-igh

The ***Baru***, or cleaver-headed crocodile, grew up to four metres long. It was more powerful than a saltwater crocodile and had 15-centimetre claws.
BAR-oo

# Did you know?

**Fossils from the Miocene help us understand how modern species evolved. Similar fossils are found at Bullock Creek in the Northern Territory and Riversleigh in Queensland.**

## WHERE ARE THEY?

A display of Alcoota fossils can be seen at Megafauna Central in Alice Springs.

***Dromornis stirtoni*** was the largest bird to ever live in Australia. It was a flightless bird called a mihirung.
DROM-oorn-is STUR-ton-igh / MEE-hee-rung

The massive beak of ***Dromornis*** may have been for cracking hard seeds and tough-skinned fruits.

# Where Lions Stalked

## MARGARET RIVER

### WHAT ARE THEY?

Megafauna are found in many places in Australia, including the caves of the Margaret River area. These caves include both extinct fossil species and evidence of early humans.

***Thylacoleo carnifex*** was a leopard-sized marsupial predator that could climb trees. THIGH-lak-oh-lee-oh KAR-ni-fex

Powerful jaws and sharp teeth for crushing and cutting prey

Large, stocky forelimbs

Semi-opposable thumb with a long, hooked claw for hunting

Flexible joints for climbing trees

### Did you know?

**You can see ancient 'living rocks' or thrombolites at Lake Clifton. Fossils of these species are 3.5 billion years old. They are the oldest living form of life on Earth.**

THROM-boh-lights

*Thylacoleo*'s blade-like back teeth were very effective for slicing through prey.

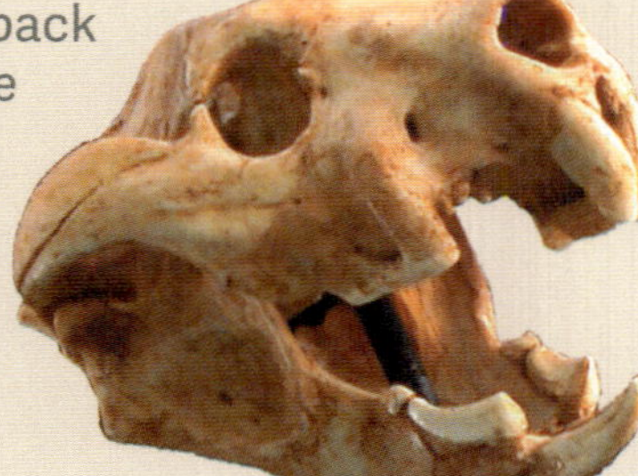

| Cambrian | Ordovician | Silurian | Devonian | Carboniferous | Permian | Triassic | Jurassic | Cretaceous | Paleogene | Neogene |
|---|---|---|---|---|---|---|---|---|---|---|

−500 million years −400 −300 −200 −100 0

***Genyornis newtoni***
was a common flightless bird that was five times heavier than an emu.
jen-ee-OOR-nis NYOO-ton-igh

Western Australia

## WHERE ARE THEY?

Margaret River is famous for its karri and marri forests and its beautiful limestone caves. Mammoth Cave is easily accessible. Lake Cave, Jewel Cave and Ngilgi Cave also have spectacular limestone and crystal decorations.

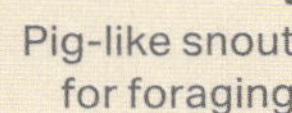


***Zygomaturus trilobus***
was a large, solitary herbivore about the size of a bull. It lived near water.
zigh-goh-MAT-yoo-rus TRIGH-loh-bus

***Zaglossus hacketti***
was a large, long-legged echidna that grew to one metre long.
zaa-GLOS-us HAK-et-igh

The giant python ***Wonambi naracoortensis*** was first found in the Naracoorte Caves but has also been found in south-west Western Australia.
WON-am-bee NAR-a-coor-TEN-sis

# More Amazing Fossils

**There are many other important fossil sites in Australia.**

1

Giant mosasaurs hunted off the coast of Western Australia.
MOH-zoh-soorz

**Bullock Creek** contains many Miocene fossils from 12 million years ago.

Dinosaur footprints can be found along the Western Australian coast from **Broome** to Carnarvon.

1 The **Gogo Formation** is a fossil reef containing many **ancient fish**.

2

2 Children found the shin bone of ***Ozraptor subotaii*** near **Geraldton** in 1966.
OZ-rap-tor

**Thylacoleo Cave** is part of Australia's longest cave system in the Nullarbor. Fossils collected when animals fell into the cave between 400,000 and 800,000 years ago.

4

The Ediacara fauna, including this leaf-like ***Rangea*** from the **Flinders Ranges**, are the oldest multi-celled animals on Earth.
ed-ee-AK-ar-aa

3

**Emu Bay** on Kangaroo Island has many **trilobites**, as well as the first predator with complex eyes, *Anomalocaris*.
TRIGH-lo-bights / an-om-AL-oh-CA-ris

**Horned tortoises** are found in Queensland and on several Pacific Islands.

Land animals, like the ankylosaur ***Kunbarrasaurus***, have also been found at **Richmond**.
ANK-lee-oh-soor / kun-ba-raa-SOOR-us

7

7

This giant amphibian, ***Xenobrachyops allos***, was found in Queensland, east of **Emerald**.
zeen-oh-BRAK-ee-ops AL-oss

6

6

5 The first Australian ankylosaur, ***Minmi paravertebra***, was found near **Roma**, Queensland, in 1964.
MIN-mee PARR-a-VUR-te-braa

5

**Lake Callabonna** in South Australia contains many remarkable megafauna fossils, as well as fossil flamingos.
KAL-aa-BON-aa

4

**Cuddie Springs** is an important Pleistocene megafauna site in New South Wales.
PLIGH-sto-seen

3

**Lancefield** is an important site for megafauna fossils in Victoria.

The fossil cliffs of **Maria Island** are filled with sea creatures from the Permian period 300 million years ago, when Australia was covered in thick ice.

When Charles Darwin visited Australia, he collected fossils near **Hobart**.

# Glossary

**amphibian** a group of cold-blooded animals, including frogs
**canine (teeth)** pointed teeth towards the front of the mouth
**carnivorous** meat-eating
**coelurosaur** a group of two-footed theropod dinosaurs
**conifer** a cone-bearing tree, including pines
**femur** thigh bone
**fossils** preserved traces of past life
**gizzard** the muscular second stomach of birds and dinosaurs, used to grind food
**Gondwana** a supercontinent made up of Australia, Antarctica, South America and Africa
**herbivorous** plant-eating
**intestine** part of the digestive system
**marine** of the sea
**marsupial** a pouch-bearing mammal
**megafauna** a group of large animals that went extinct 40,000 – 50,000 years ago
**mekosuchine** an extinct group of crocodiles
**molar** a grinding tooth at the back of the mouth
**opal** a gemstone that often contains fossils
**ornithischian** one of two types of dinosaurs characterised by bird-like hips
**ornithopod** a group of two-footed ornithischian dinosaurs
**polar** of the North or South Pole
**predator** a hunter, meat-eater
**protruding** sticking out
**rift valley** a low, flat area caused by two landmasses moving apart
**saurischian** one of two types of dinosaurs characterised by lizard-like hips
**sauropod** a group of large four-footed saurischian dinosaurs
**temnospondyl** an extinct group of large predatory amphibians
**theropod** a group of meat-eating saurischian dinosaurs that mostly walked on their hind legs

# Places to Go

### NEW SOUTH WALES
Age of Fishes Museum, Canowindra
Australian Museum, Sydney

### NORTHERN TERRITORY
Megafauna Central, Alice Springs
The Museum and Art Gallery of the Northern Territory, Darwin

### QUEENSLAND
Australian Age of Dinosaurs Museum, Winton
Eromanga Natural History Museum, Eromanga
Kronosaurus Korner, Richmond
Queensland Museum, Brisbane
Riversleigh Fossil Centre, Mount Isa
Dinosaur Stampede National Monument, Lark Quarry Conservation Park, near Winton

### SOUTH AUSTRALIA
South Australian Museum, Adelaide
Wonambi Fossil Centre, Naracoorte Caves

### TASMANIA
Tasmanian Museum and Art Gallery, Hobart

### VICTORIA
Bunurong Environment Centre, Inverloch
Melbourne Museum

### WESTERN AUSTRALIA
Western Australian Museum, Perth

**You can discover more about prehistoric animals at these museums and fossil centres. Not all the fossil sites in this book have their own museums or information centres but you can still visit the sites, tour the caves or look at ancient dinosaur footprints, depending on which site you are visiting.**

# Index of Animals

# Picture Credits

**Cover**
*Ozraptor subotaii*. Artist: Xing Lida / *Australian Geographic*
*Diprotodon optatum* (detail). Artist: Peter Trusler. Courtesy Australia Post

**Page ii** *Thylacoleo carnifex*. Artist: Mauricio Anton

**Amazing Australian Fossils**
Timeline. Based on a timeline created by David Meagher
Geological map. Based on data from Geoscience Australia. Artist: Danielle Clode
Stromatolites at Carbla Point, Shark Bay, Western Australia. Photographer: Malcolm Wallace

**Fossicking for Fossils**
Fossil formation graphic. By Danielle Clode. Based on illustrations by T Saxby, K Kraeer and L Van Essen, from the IAN Image Library (http://ian.umces.edu/imagelibrary/)
*Thylacoleo* skull, Naracoorte, South Australia. Photographer: John Long
A *Diprotodon* skeleton exposed on the surface of a clay pan at Lake Callabonna, South Australia. Photographer: Aaron Camens
Tetrapod trackways. Photographer: Peter Nearhos. © Museums Victoria
Sea-cliff fossils, Maria Island, Tasmania. Photographer: Stephanie Sykora
Insect in amber. Photographer: John Broomfield. © Museums Victoria

**The Age of Megafauna: Naracoorte Caves**
*Diprotodon optatum* (detail). Artist: Peter Trusler. Courtesy Australia Post
*Procoptodon goliah* (detail). Artist: Peter Trusler. Courtesy Australia Post
*Palorchestes azael*. Artist: Peter Trusler
*Latagallina naracoortensis*. Based on a malleefowl photograph by Butupa. Adapted under creative commons by Elen Shute and Danielle Clode
*Propleopus oscillans*. Artist: Frank Knight. From P Vickers-Rich and G van Tets, *Kadimakara*. © P Vickers-Rich
*Diprotodon* skull. Photographer: Rodney Start. © Museums Victoria

**Polar Dinosaurs: Dinosaur Cove**
*Leaellynasaura amicagraphica* (detail). Artist: Peter Trusler. Courtesy Australia Post
*Qantassaurus intrepidus* (detail). Artist: Peter Trusler
*Atlascopcosaurus loadsi*. Artist: Andrew Plant
*Eryops megacephalus* (cast). Photographer: Gunnar Creutz (http://creativecommons.org/licenses/by-sa/4.0), [deep-etched version]
*Bishops whitmorei* (detail). Artist: Peter Trusler
*Leaellynasaura* brain case. Photographer: Steve Morton

**Ancient Whales and Deadly Dolphins: Torquay Coast**
*Janjucetus hunderi*. Artist: Carl Buell
*Mammalodon colliveri*. Artist: Carl Buell
*Prosqualodon*. Artist: Carl Buell
*Waipatiid* dolphin. Artist: Carl Buell
*Janjucetus hunderi* skull (cast). Model-maker: Kym Haines. Photographer: Jon Augier. © Museums Victoria

**Giant Sharks and Toothy Birds: Beaumaris**
*Livyatan* (detail). Artist: Brian Choo
*Carcharocles megalodon*. Courtesy of Smithsonian Institution. Artist: M Parrish
*Pelagornis*. Artist: Peter Trusler
*Pseudaptenodytes macraei* (detail). Artist: Peter Trusler

*Carcharocles megalodon* tooth. Photographer: Rodney Start. © Museums Victoria
Fossilised tooth of Killer sperm whale between tooth of *Tyrannosaurus rex* (left) and modern whale (right). Photographer: Benjamin Healley. © Museums Victoria

**Caves of Prehistoric Giants: Wellington Caves**
*Varanus priscus* (*Megalania*) (detail). Artist: Peter Trusler. Courtesy Australia Post
*Bohra paulae*. Artist: Peter Schouten
*Phascolonus gigas*. Artist: Peter Schouten
*Sarcophilus harrisii* (Tasmanian devil). Photographer: Ian McCann. © Museums Victoria
*Diprotodon* skeleton (cast). Photographer: John Broomfield. © Museums Victoria

**The Lake of Armoured Fish: Canowindra**
*Mandageria fairfaxi*. Courtesy of the Age of Fishes Museum
*Groenlandaspis*. Courtesy of the Age of Fishes Museum
*Bothriolepis yeungae*. Courtesy of the Age of Fishes Museum
*Remigolepis walkeri*. Courtesy of the Age of Fishes Museum
Photograph of fish fossil bed. Photographer: Kim Lau

**Dinosaurs of Lightning Claws: Lightning Ridge**
Megaraptor 'Lightning Claw'. Courtesy Phil Bell
*Muttaburrasaurus langdoni* (detail). Artist: Peter Trusler. Courtesy Australia Post
*Neoceratodus forsteri*. Artist: Frank Knight. From P Vickers-Rich and G van Tets, *Kadimakara*. Copyright P Vickers-Rich
*Steropodon galmani*. Artist: Peter Schouten
Ornithopod feeding. © Queensland Museum, Vlad Konstantinov, Andrey Atuchin, Scott Hocknull
*Kollikodon ritchiei* teeth. Courtesy: Australian Museum

**Thingodonts and Fangaroos: Riversleigh**
*Balbaroo fangaroo*. Artist: Peter Schouten
*Yalkaparidon coheni*. Artist: Filipe Martinho
*Emuary*. Artist: Peter Schouten
*Ekaltadeta*. Artist: Peter Schouten
Nimiokoala. Artist: Peter Schouten
*Yarala burchfieldi* bandicoot skull. Reproduced from Warburton and Travouillon (2016), with permission from CSIRO Publishing

**The Mighty Titanosaurs: Eromanga**
*Titanosaur*. Source: Eromanga Natural History Museum. Creator: Andrey Atuchin
Plant images. Artist: Danielle Clode
Sauropod footprint. Photographer: Dianne Bennett
Femur bones. Source: Eromanga Natural History Museum. Creator: Vlad Konstantinov

**Megaraptors and the Big Stampede: Winton**
*Australovenator wintonensis*. Artist Xing Lida/Australian Geographic
*Diamantinasaurus matildae*. Artist: Travis Tischler © Australian Age of Dinosaurs Ltd
*Isisfordia*. Artist: Matt Herne
Theropod. © Queensland Museum, Vlad Konstantinov, Andrey Atuchin, Scott Hocknull
Lark Quarry footprints. © Queensland Museum, Gary Cranitch

**Beasts of the Inland Sea: Hughenden and Richmond**
*Kronosaurus queenslandicus*. Artist: Xing Lida / *Australian Geographic*
*Platypterygius longmani*. Artist: Xing Lida / *Australian Geographic*
*Eromangasaurus australis*. Artist: Josh Lee, Adelaide. From *Dinosaurs in Australia: Mesozoic life from the southern continent* by Benjamin P Kear & Robert J Hamilton-Bruce
Pterasaur skeleton (detail). Illustrator: Cally Bennett. © Museums Victoria
Ammonite (model). Photographer: Andrew Curtis. © Museums Victoria
Belemnite. Model-maker: Peter Roberts. Photographer: Jon Augier. © Museums Victoria
Belemnite guard. Photographer: Rodney Start. © Museums Victoria

**Life with the Thunderbirds: Alcoota**
*Dromornis stirtoni* skeleton. © Museum and Art Gallery of the Northern Territory
*Dromornis* (detail). Artist. Peter Trusler
*Wakaleo vanderleuri*. Artist: Peter Schouten
*Kolopsis torus*. Artist: Peter Schouten
*Palorchestes painei*. Artist: Dr Cahue Sbrana
*Baru darrowi*. Artist: Anne Musser. © Australian Museum
*Dromornis* skull. © Museum and Art Gallery of the Northern Territory

**Where Lions Stalked: Margaret River**
*Thylacoleo carnifex*. Artist: Mauricio Anton
*Zygomaturus trilobus*. Artist: Peter Schouten
*Wonambi naracoortensis*. Artist: Frank Knight. From P Vickers-Rich and G van Tets, Kadimakara. © P Vickers-Rich
*Genyornis newtoni* (detail). Artist: Peter Trusler. Courtesy Australia Post
*Zaglossus hacketti*. Artist: Peter Schouten
Thylacoleo skull. Courtesy Rod Wells

**More Amazing Fossils**
*Ediacara* fauna. Artist: Lauren Nicholls
Map by studioether
Gogo fish. Artist: John Long
*Minmi paravertebra*. Artist: Peter Trusler. Courtesy Australia Post
*Kunbarrasaurus*. © Queensland Museum, Vlad Konstantinov, Andrew Atuchin Scott Hucknull
*Xenobrachyops allos*. © Queensland Museum, Vlad Konstantinov, Andrey Atuchin, Scott Hocknull
Horned tortoise skeleton. Photographer: J Fields. Courtesy Australian Museum
Trilobite. Model-maker: Tom Davies. Photographer: Benjamin Healley. © Museums Victoria
*Ozraptor subotaii*. Artist: Xing Lida / *Australian Geographic*

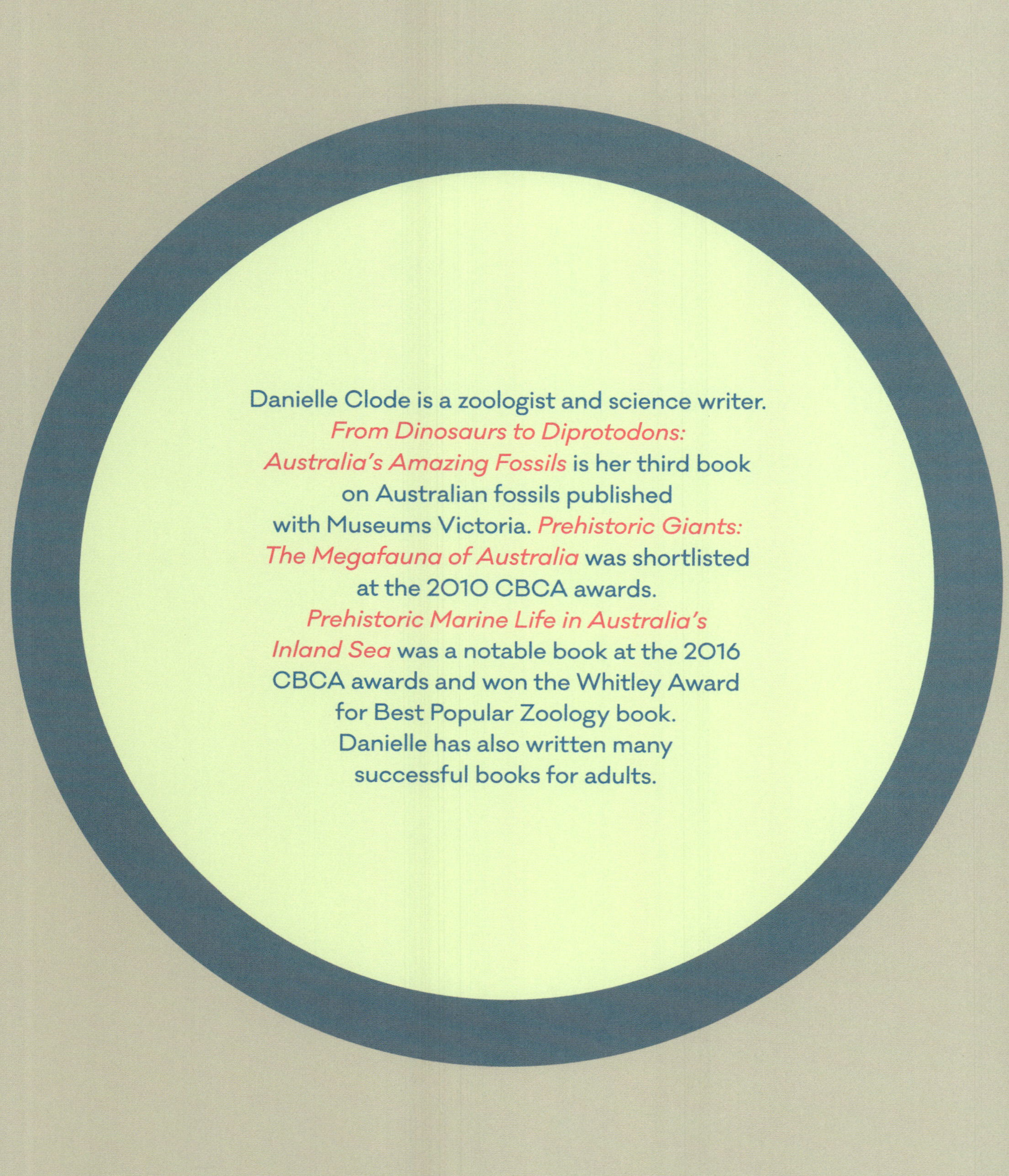

Danielle Clode is a zoologist and science writer. *From Dinosaurs to Diprotodons: Australia's Amazing Fossils* is her third book on Australian fossils published with Museums Victoria. *Prehistoric Giants: The Megafauna of Australia* was shortlisted at the 2010 CBCA awards. *Prehistoric Marine Life in Australia's Inland Sea* was a notable book at the 2016 CBCA awards and won the Whitley Award for Best Popular Zoology book. Danielle has also written many successful books for adults.

**Acknowledgements**
Thanks to Melanie Raymond and her publishing team for proposing and producing this book. We're also grateful to all of the palaeontologists, palaeo-artists and editors who commented on and corrected aspects of this book and who provided images and advice. We'd particularly like to thank Marija Bacic, Phil Bell, Aaron Camens, Erich Fitzgerald, Brenda Gurr, John Long, Sally Rogers-Davidson, Rolf Schmidt, Elen Shute, Rod Wells and Tim Ziegler.

First published by Museums Victoria Publishing in 2018
Reprinted 2019, 2024

Designed by Elizabeth Dias, studioether
Printed in China by RR Donnelley Asia Printing Solutions, Ltd.
Museums Victoria Publishing
11 Nicholson Street, Carlton, Victoria 3053, Australia
publications@museum.vic.gov.au
www.museumsvictoria.com.au

A catalogue record for this book is available from the National Library of Australia